Much More Than Love

Vritika Rene Viswanathan

Copyright © 2022 by Vritika Rene Viswanathan

All rights reserved. This book or any portion thereof may not be reproduced or used in any manner whatsoever without the express written permission of the respective writer of the respective poem/story except for the use of brief quotations in a book review. The writer of the respective work holds sole responsibility for the originality of the poems/stories and The Write Order is not responsible in any way whatsoever.

Illustrations are drawn by the author herself.

Printed in India

ISBN: 978-93-95079-45-7

First Printing, 2022

The Write Order
Koramangala, Bangalore

Karnataka- 560029

THE WRITE ORDER PUBLICATIONS.

www.thewriteorder.com

Thanks to

My Grandfather for always inspiring me

and

Varsha Aunty for being my mentor

Author's Note

My experience is not exceptional, but it is important. Adoptees want you to know that their experience is authentic and that no one can "correct" it. Seeing their children struggle with the difficulties of adoption is challenging for parents. Parents will never be able to take away their child's pain from his or her past experiences. They can, however, provide a secure environment for their child to express current feelings regarding adoption at various stages of life, allowing them to better integrate the experience. The adoptee wants and needs to have their feelings validated, as well as a loving presence.

Hold my hand

And walk with me

But at my pace

Till you understand my true anxiety

Hold my hand

As I swim so blindly

Full of emotions flooding the surface

Hold me

Through my fear and depression

Hold my hand

For this ride

Hold me tight for

This roller-coaster may take some time

Hold my hand

As I learn and unlearn

Hold me

Even when I am at peace

For letting go is not something

That comes with such ease

Hold my hand

For my serenity

Hold me and understand me

Till I finally find my identity

Prologue

I am a 14-year-old teenager. This is my narrative. I'll speak about my experience growing up as an adopted child. All of the highs and lows I've experienced, as well as how I've felt up to this point.

I was adopted as an infant. My parents revealed this information when I was nine years old. Since then, I've noticed drastic changes in my behaviour and my outlook.

I am sure other adopted kids going through similar situations, to what I'm going through, would be able to relate to what I'm feeling or going through.

In this narrative, by revisiting my past, I have had an amazing time interacting with my family and friends, learning, and appreciating some forgotten memories and humbled by the love, affection and guidance that I have received in my journey so far.

This book is also for my own benefit. I'm analysing myself. Since a chat with my Grandfather, I've been fascinated by psychology and transactional analysis. This started the thought process of following this path for self-analysis. I believe that transactional analysis could benefit me and direct me to the right path, in the process of creating this book, and that conducting this analysis would assist to clarify my behaviour as a whole.

I chose to write the narrative first and later part the psycho-analytical evaluations, so as to not break the interest of young readers.

My personal narrative helped me understand myself better and helped me create a base to work on myself for my well being.

Teenagers already go through insecurities and other common problems during this phase of their life. Being an adopted child does not help and all these negative feelings get amplified.

This narrative would help the community understand why we act the way we do, as well as parents realise the issues we face as adopted children.

Each chapter is based on my memories of significant events in my life and as told to me by my family. I'll use the material in each chapter to figure out what life situation I was in at the time. I'll also be analysing my current life position and determining how I might shift my life position to "I'm OK, you're OK."

TABLE OF CONTENTS

PART -I 6

Chapter 1 Jab We Met 8

Chapter 2 Under The Weather Forever 16

Chapter 3 Jab Hum Chotey Thei 26

PART -II 34

Chapter 4 Abrupt Disclosure 36

Chapter 5 That Sarcastic Kid 44

Chapter 6 Lacuna 52

Chapter 7 Burgeon 58

PART -III 64

Chapter 8 Introduction to TA 66

Chapter 9 Self-Analysis 80

Epilogue 107

About The Author 109

Bibliography 111

PART -I

UTOPIAN WORLD

Chapter 1
Jab We Met

It was the Universe conspiring

Powering the magnetic forces

A Rendezvous with fate

Then we met...

I t was that time of the year when the monsoon slowly fades away and the whole of Kerala is a canvas with a pantone of exuberant greens. On that fateful day, the clouds were clapping, and the water droplets were dancing in a trance as they hit the ground. That was the day when my family met me for the very first time.

Truly, nature had helped me make a rather spectacular entrance. After all this was when they met the goddess of mischief...

OK!! This may not be exactly how it would have happened, but let's just roll with this for the sake of my freedom of thought...Let's be honest here, no one really remembers the settings.

That life changing morning, in Coimbatore, my Grandfather received a phone call and was informed that there was a baby for adoption and that they could come have a visit. It was an eight-hour long drive to the orphanage. My grandparents and my uncle (whom I lovingly call Romama) arrived there mid-afternoon.

My Grandmother recalls hearing children learning rhymes and the classic classroom banter, as she entered the orphanage. She vividly remembers that there were staff taking care of toddlers and a staff member calling out to Indira trying to get her attention.

Little did she know that Indira was going to be a massive part of her life...

It was love at first sight, from what I heard. I was a tiny girl with a massive smile, kind big eyes and with a runny nose. Apparently, I was really energetic, and I wanted to interact with these three people, who were smiling non-stop. My connection was instantaneous with my uncle. When someone held me, I would turn around and focus on my uncle with a cheeky smile. He had my undivided attention. Whenever I heard his voice, I would start giggling. To this day, he still cracks me up!

My Grandmother mostly recalls wiping my flowy runny nose during the majority of the time she held me. My Grandfather and I shared a vibe and at that moment he knew that this fragile little angel would be a part of their life forever.

They, then, called my parents who were still in Dubai as they weren't able to take time off from work to visit me. I spoke to my Father first, it was gibberish, but I did speak a lot (the irony is that I was an introvert later...LOL). This was our TÊTE-à-TÊTE. I guess they were too enamoured by my charming self and were already in love with me to know that I was the ONE.

My parents finally managed to get a week off and flew down to visit me at the orphanage. From what I am told, my Father would never let go off me once he took me in his arms. Though I was in his arms, I would, with those tiny hands of mine, hold on to my Mother's fingers. I still do the same, especially when my mom has food in her hand!

My Father wouldn't stop kissing me and hugging me... Ugh! I still have to keep away! I had an uncanny resemblance to my Father and that amazed everyone.

After a while, I slept on my Mother's chest with my head nuzzled into her neck. I have always slept by my Mothers' side when I was tiny.... Who am I kidding! I still do... But let's clarify this, she is the one who is scared of the darkness, not me!

After this visit, they couldn't keep away, thus leading to frequent visits. We have a close-knit family, and I was always having visitors from different uncles, aunts and cousins. This happened for three whole months as the paperwork, as usual, took a lot of time.

One day my Grandfather received a call from the orphanage director. He had a special request. There had been a scabies outbreak in the orphanage and all the kids were infected. They were finding it difficult containing the outbreak.

As my health condition was worrisome, they had come up with the decision to hand me over to my grandparents, so that I could get better individual care. This was not normally done, as the child is usually handed over to the parents only after the paperwork was completed. Technically so...my grandparents became my first foster parents.

On receiving the call, my grandparents were overjoyed and readily agreed. They, along with Pravin Uncle's family rushed there the very next day. There was a prayer ceremony to hand over the child, which was solemn and touching. My grandparents confessed that tear-drops were rolling down their cheeks during the entire ceremony.

It was a long drive to my grandparents' house at Coimbatore. I played with my cousin for some parts of the journey and blissfully slept throughout the rest of the journey on my Grandmother's lap. On reaching home, my grandparents had a small homecoming ceremony with a traditional lamp lighting and prayer.

I am told that I adapted to new surroundings pretty well. Of course! I was finally with my family...

Chapter 2
Under The Weather Forever

I am told that I adapted to new surroundings pretty well. Of course! I was finally with my family...

Chapter 2
Under The Weather Forever

A moment in time so pensive

Perhaps an illumination of strength

Through the pains she evolved

A resilient phoenix...

According to the documents received from the orphanage, I was diagnosed with pneumonia four times off and on until I was four months old. I was constantly hospitalised, and my diet was supplemented with antibiotics. Maybe it was because of all these medicines or loss of appetite that I had listless blonde/ greyish hair. Which I must say I did indeed pull off. And currently, I have luscious black hair with maroon highlights which people are extremely jealous of. When I was brought to my Grandparent's home, I was already infected with scabies. I had rashes all over my body and severe itching, which I was too small to react to. It was at the time when my parents were still getting the paperwork done and arranging for the passport to take me with them to Dubai. It was also not advisable to take a scabies infested child to Dubai, as it would be difficult to contain its spread.

My grandparents had to struggle a lot during the first month since I had scabies. Everything that I touched was sterilised with hot water. As this could not be done in a modern kitchen, my grandparents made a hearth (*chulha*), got firewood and huge vessels. Every morning they used to sterilise my clothes, toys, sheets and curtains. They also ended up contracting scabies from me.

I am extremely lucky to have a family filled with doctors. It took a month for the 3 of us to recover from scabies. My aunt Geetha, who is a dermatologist, used to prescribe the medicines needed for recovery from Kozhikode. My uncle Rohit(Romama), who is a Gastro

Surgeon, used to travel during weekends to check on me and my progress. My uncle had a two-year-old child (my cousin Adi). My uncle had no intention of infesting him with scabies. Every weekend after my uncle visited me, he would apply the scabies medicine all over himself, travel all the way back like that and used to wash off the medicine once reaching his house. This was the only reason my cousin wasn't infected. I can only imagine the amount of pain everyone had gone through to get me to recover and how hectic it must've been.

Once I was scabies free my mom had then taken a week off to come visit me. By then I was 8 months old, potty trained and running around causing havoc. It had taken 2 long months for the completion of the paperwork.

It was then my parents came down from Dubai. My name was then changed from Indira to my present lovely name... thank goodness for that. My parents had a massive name changing ceremony, that was when I met the whole squad AKA my family. They took me to Dubai with them after the ceremony.

I was mostly sick in Dubai, either with the flu or a common cold. And every second month I was under the weather. I was often on antibiotics and a couple of other medicines as well, which meant that my medicine cabinet was always full. I was told that I had colourful medicines. *"Thank god for small mercies."*

At the age of 2 my usual cold didn't subside for a while and had swelling around my eyes. Keep in mind that I was a scrawny kid with bulging eyes. My Mother described me as her E.T. child. The casual visit to the doc ended up with some quite appalling news. I was diagnosed with nephrotic syndrome. Even I don't know what it meant, so I did my share of investigation (bugging my mom) and here's the gist of what I understood:

"*Nephrotic syndrome is a rare chronic disease. This means that the kidney causes my body to excrete too much protein. Being a chronic disease, this also meant that this could stick with me for many years together or may be lifelong.*"

I was admitted in the hospital for 10 days. After the tenth day the doctors asked my parents to take me home and continue the treatment there as the treatment would take quite a bit of time. The doctor then gave instructions to my parents on how to go about the procedure at home and how to monitor me. My urine samples were tested for protein every day on a routine basis. I was already on steroids and other tablets which would continue for almost a whole year. Steroids turned the scrawny kid into a fat, obese moon-faced kid, as this was one of the major side effects of having steroids. I was put on a no salt and no carbs diet. *This is surprising because I can't live without either of those now.* My mom told me that she used to grind broccoli, boiled fish and eggs in a mixer and feed it to me in the form of a smoothie. *This should explain why I'm not fond of smoothies now.* I honestly have no idea how I managed to survive through that, the diet still scares me till' this day. Blech!

This continued for 6 months which was until my urine strip showed negative protein output. The steroid was tapered off for the next 6 months. I'm currently still in remission and I'm extremely lucky that it hasn't resurfaced until now. I had joined school soon after this ailment. Since I was still on steroids which was being slowly tapered off, my immunity was low. I used to be the first to catch a flu or anything that was in the air for that matter. Though I was a chubby healthy-looking child, I continued to be under the weather for the next horrendous 3 years.

I was six, when I was struck by lightning once again…This was during the period when I had caught the flu three times in a row. I was on heavy antibiotics and the dosage was increased every time I fell sick. The dosage had to be increased as any sort of severe infection could lead to my nephrotic syndrome to resurface. I started noticing blisters in my mouth which started off as one or two but then progressed to cover the inside of my mouth entirely. I wasn't able to eat or drink anything. There was continuous pus oozing from my mouth. Three doctors collaborated with each other from different hospitals and came to a conclusion and diagnosed it as *oral herpes.* So, I was back to the hospital but this time for 14 days in the isolation ward with my Mother. I was continuously on drips. Both my arms were swollen and painful because of the drips and the injections. Even after 14 days there was no progress in my condition. That's when my Mother decided to take me back home to India.

As I have mentioned earlier my family is filled with doctors and my Mother felt that moral support was indeed needed as I had gone almost 15 days without a morsel of food or water, other than the fluids which were given intravenously through the drips. Once I had reached India, my aunt Geetha suggested a doctor which led me to be admitted in a hospital here, again. The doctor then did a biopsy of my blister and ruled out herpes. My aunt and the doctor then diagnosed my ailment as Behcet Syndrome and then they put me under the required treatment which meant along with new medicines, I was again back on steroids. *Inspector Rene back on duty.* I did a little digging on this topic (again bugging my Mother) and here is the gist of the disease:

"It is a very rare disease which is also chronic. Oh, the irony! It seems this time my immune system was attacking my healthy tissues."

On the 25th day I was able to drink water and the 26th day I had my first solid meal. This roller coaster of ailments perturbed my parents, especially my Father. He didn't want me to be dragged down by all these ailments. So, he enrolled me into a sport. He wanted me to make fitness a way of my life. My Father decided on tennis as he adored the game….still does. Tennis became my getaway and helped me channel my energy positively. This really did help bring a healthy lifestyle which indeed helped keep these ailments in remission.These ailments were a big part of my childhood. But, these illnesses did not define my childhood in entirety.

There was so much more to it...

Chapter 3
Jab Hum Chotey Thei

This little girl met the world

With only the power of opinion

She put her foot down and stayed strong

And never did she frown...

Apart from those under the weather days, I lead a pretty normal childhood.

I have a security blanket with me. I always have it with me. It's not usual for people to have such tendencies, but as I already stated, I'm different. When I have my blanket, I find comfort because it keeps me warm and secure. It's one thing to have a security blanket, but it's quite another to go insane without one. When I lose it or misplace it, I experience a panic episode *which is practically me before every Math exam*. My parents tried their best to get rid of this habit, but in vain. So, they decided to cut the blanket into handkerchief size, so that it could be cleaned often and is portable.

I was dyslexic, although the intensity was not much. I used to mix up words and letters and wouldn't grasp things fast. I used to flip the numbers, like; 54 used to turn into 45. But after some time I had gotten over this.

When I was in kindergarten, I wasn't that mischievous, but I was very definite of my wants and no amount of persuasion could change that. Obviously, all of my decisions as a child were made in good faith. My teacher had described me as someone that was very clear about what she wanted and that she did not look to others for guidance, nor did she seek approval from others. Basically, this means when others were choosing a certain colour pencil because of their peers, I chose the colour pencil I wanted and did not let anyone influence my decision.

I can do a lot for my friends, including punching a guy twice my size. True story! Because he was picking on my pal, I punched a bully who was one grade senior to me. Yes, I can be a great friend; but my compulsive urge to lead the team can make me appear needy at times. No one likes a needy buddy. I was always convinced that I was correct, and I needed others to agree with me. If things didn't work out, I would start a fight. To put it another way, I guess I was a bully. I used to pick on others by insulting them or pushing them to do things they didn't want to, such as play games that I made up. I used to make up games to entertain my pals, but they were never entertained. They would leave me and go play with others, and I would wonder why.

I've always stood by my mates. As a friend, I believe it is the least I can do. Even if my pals abandoned me when I needed them, I've always been there for them. I don't particularly like this aspect of myself, but I might as well embrace it. I'm a misunderstood person. I'm not the type who leaves in any circumstance. Yes, I have a flight response from time to time, but it's usually because I don't want to deal with any foolishness at the time. I'm not someone who is afraid of taking risks. When the cops came to speak to my Father as he was pulled over, I recall being by his side. All my friends took my arm and ran away on seeing the cops. But as I was running, I realised my Father was alone, so I turned back and stood by my Father, gazing directly into the cops' eyes, showing no trace of weakness. It was the bare minimum I could do.

I'm now an ambivert, and I was once informed that I was the most introverted child. I used to feel apprehensive of being in a gathering. I was told I was always quiet and sat in the corner or would cling on to my parents. My parents tell me that I used to get hassled on hearing loud music, the irony, now my Mother has to scream to get me to turn down the music. I was, like forever, in a phase where I considered myself a boy, until recently. It was my assumption that girls were always pretty and I never considered myself to be attractive. I felt like I could relate to boys more visually then. I disliked the stereotype "very girly," games most girls played. I'm referring to dress up and playtime with Barbie dolls. I preferred playing a sport or one of my "boring" made up games. *I was creative, gotta give that to me.*

I've always been a brave soul and an adventure seeker, who enjoyed trying new things, such as a new ride at the mall which others would hesitate to go on. I was so motivated to do anything and everything I wanted that even if I was terrified, I would go ahead and do it. I had even gone on a skydiving simulator. They would place us in a tube and let heavy wind from the turbines flow under the tube which would lift the person up and give a feeling of flying in the air. It was one of the most incredible experiences I'd ever had, and despite my fears, I went forward with my decision, which is pretty awesome considering I was just 6 years old at that time!

I am a huge animal lover. I love animals of any kind (except spiders). Humans, on the other hand, do not appeal much to me. I am primarily concerned about animals. I've cared for sick animals even when I was a toddler. I care for animals especially when they're vulnerable and in desperate need of assistance. It's become a way of life for me; whenever I see an animal, I feel compelled to aid them and nurture them back to health. I must have 'inherited' this quality from my Grandfather. He's taken in a lot of animals, including squirrels, and nursed them back to health. After experiencing the thrill of assisting an injured animal for the first time, I craved more of the same. Not to always put myself on the pedestal, but I would like to also say that I was a big drama queen. For that I would have to write about another weird condition that I had. I used to frequently dislocate my hand, it could be my shoulders, my elbow or my wrists. I used to dislocate my elbow by any jolt or even by dancing or flailing my arm. It was excruciatingly uncomfortable. I realised that when I dislocated my arm, I used to be able to slack off or get what I wanted. Here, I have to admit that I am a fantastic actress and I am quite proud of it. My Mother on the other hand would beg to differ as she had to deal with my tantrums. I still remember, I had gone to a toy store in a mall (like any kid would) and didn't want to leave (like any other kid would). My family, however, wanted to go home. We were running late, so my grandma grabbed my hand to hurry me out of the store. I yelped and wailed. My Grandmother was shocked that she had hurt me by causing my wrist to dislocate. For the next few days, I pretended that my wrist was hurting in order to get favours from my grandma. On the third day, my friend brought over balloons and out of excitement I started playing with them, totally forgetting about my wrist pain. It was at this moment my Grandmother knew what I was up to for the last 3 days.

Another pet peeve that I have is my aversion to the word "no". It irritates me to no end! It could make me throw a tantrum and I would immediately stop listening to any logic. I guess it made me feel weak and insignificant which is not something I want to be. It's strange that I'm like this. I'm well aware of this. It's just that someone saying anything awful like "no" would make me respond irrationally. When my aunties or uncles said the word "no" to me, I recall yanking out a handful of my Mother's hair. Another example of mayhem is when I threw a fit in the subway after my uncle said "no." In a sense, I was hurt. I had made up my mind to stay on the metro and not get off at all. On the other hand, this terrified my uncle, and let's face it, we'd all learnt our lesson. Yes, the word "no" has wreaked havoc.

I'm not a big fan of the statement "I hate you," but it doesn't bother me as much. It could be that I'm extremely sensitive. See, I'm not the type to provoke. I'm incredibly irritable, and I can quickly turn something insignificant into something massive. Yes, I am prone to overthinking and overreacting. We are just getting into that part of my story where the drama unfolds.

PART -II

STRUCK BY LIGHTNING

Chapter 4
Abrupt Disclosure

The blue sky gradually being obscured

The grey clouds bringing gloom

A storm began to brew,

Disrupting the peace

And it was then that

The lightning struck...

How I was told that I was adopted ….(DUN DUNNN!!!)

On that eventful day, there were bombs flying and people were yelling out for protection. It was horrific and weirdly in slow-motion. OK… OK… I know I exaggerated a **tiny** bit there, but it definitely felt like war inside me.

So, this is how THE story actually went; That evening, I was hanging out with my friends not knowing that in a few minutes from now my entire understanding of life would change.

My favourite cousin Adi (no offense to my other cousins…I love you all too!) was visiting us and I was to accompany my Father to pick him up from the Railway Station in a while. So, I decided to head back home as I had already received calls, twice, from my Father asking me to come back home.

But my parents had different plans. They said that they need to talk to me about something very important. They were acting abnormal and my mind started to think of all the possible mischievous things I could have done to warrant this meeting.

They asked me to sit me down… *strange*, then my Father made me lie down on his lap… *strange again!* The first few words that came out of my Father's mouth were, "You know when there is a boy and a girl…"

My eyes popped out. I was instantly embarrassed and reluctant to proceed with this conversation as I thought he was giving me **'the**

talk'. Before I could stop him, I could see my Mother rolling her eyes at my Father from my peripheral vision. My mom poked my dad to shush him.

My mom then went on to say that some babies are stomach babies and some heart babies. That very instant I realised that I was adopted. I jumped up from the sofa and screamed, "Oh, SHIT! I'm adopted!." Crying, my next instinct was to turn to my dog and say, "Cuddles, you're adopted."

There was immediately a plethora of emotions that attacked me from all the sides. A lot of questions rushed into my mind, not knowing which ones I needed the answer for first. My parents let me be. They gave me the space to absorb this bomb that they had decided to detonate on me.

After a while, I looked at my mom with disbelief and said, "Why now?." I did not care for the answer and continued, "Do you know my birth Mother?." I could see my mom shaking her head denying. I went up to her and she hugged me. I started weeping all over again.

My mind raced up to the thought of my cousin who was coming in. Maybe he knew about this. Maybe he knew all along and did not bother to tell me. He tells me everything!! How could he hide something like this from me? I seemed to be more offended by that thought. My next question to my mom was, "Does Adi know about this?," which she again denied. I asked my Mother if I could tell Adi about this, for which my mom answered, "It's your choice beta, you decide." I went up to my Father and asked him to immediately call up Romama to find out where they had reached.

I remember vividly, my Father was still sitting, looking more shocked than me at that time. He was expecting me to ask them more questions and my silence was killing him. He tried to hug me and like always I shooed him away, saying I am ok... *just call them!* By then I heard a cab pulling to a halt.

I ran out and grabbed Adi, pulling him to my room upstairs. As I reached the stairwell, I told him I am adopted. His epic reply was "*Adipoli* (awesome)." My mind went "wooooaah this dude was chill." But in reality, he thought I was pranking him like I usually do. He rushed back to my mom and asked her if what I had said was true. He had more questions to ask than me at that moment.

My Mother later informed me that they had wished to tell me sooner. But I had been dealing with more serious issues like illness, relocation to India and they felt that this was too big of an emotion to deal with at that time. They waited for me to settle down here and I was ailment free for a year when this grenade was *thrown* at me.

Chapter 5
That Sarcastic Kid

A vulnerable little girl

And so fragile

Afraid of being wounded

Put a shield around her

Chose the path of satire

Little did my parents know that there is no time known as a good time to divulge to a child that she is adopted.

Being ailment free did not mean that I was OK.

It was just a few months since we had relocated from Dubai to India. I was just getting my bearings steady. I was not yet accustomed to the non-tissue culture. How was I supposed to comprehend such a huge life changing news?

From the time we had come to India, I had not made a single friend. I was feeling left out. Language was a huge barrier for me. I felt moving was a big change and I kinda hate changes in any form. I created a racket when the refrigerator was shifted from its usual position, and here, I had moved to a very unfamiliar place... and was trying to adjust to my surroundings. It was pretty hard considering I had no friends.

I was still in the being boy phase and would try to make friends with the boys in my neighbourhood and in my school. But, when you are a boy during that age in your life where you hate girls, this was not an easy task and an unfortunate for me.

However much I tried, to please them, mainly by getting them their favourite food, they would turn on me. And with the present state of mind I was in, I was also facing another form of rejection.

I was trying not to think that my birth Mother had rejected me, though my parents had told me that she wanted the best for me, and it must have been tough for her to make this tough decision. So, at this time any such rejection would make me feel very insecure. I would then try to cling on to them more which would further drive them away.

This also was the period when I was trying to figure out how India worked, My Father, on the other hand, was trying to get his new business up and running. It was a very stressful time, and that stress was brought home, which meant there were a lot of fights at home.

This startled me and affected me drastically. I would dread that I would lose this family too. I would worry about my future and though my parents didn't love me less, I would feel very lonely, and my insecurities just kept increasing.

I began to understand how to use the power of humour and sarcasm to channel my anger or any other emotion in order to stonewall people from knowing my real feelings. I was always known as the kid with anger issues or, on occasions, the humorous kid.

The problem is that they always expect you to be hilarious. You will never be taken seriously. People frequently make these assumptions about me, but if you know me well, you will know that these preconceptions are unfounded.

I had become a lot more serious. I felt like this was my cue to grow up and to stop being a child. This also had me worried about everything. By everything, I literally mean everything! I overthought everything. I was also majorly insecure at this time, which led me to become a pushover and a people pleaser.

This was the worst time I had gone through (including all my sickness times as well). I felt like I was an alien among them. Then I started to exclude myself from any sort of gatherings and remained grumpy.

I could see subtle changes in my character. I had, from a cheerful kid to a sassy *Garfield*, become *Grumpy* the dwarf (my growth spurt was yet to happen)... It still hasn't happened... who am I kidding!

My defence mechanism was sarcasm.

Perhaps, it's because I tend to live in the realm of television and living in that make-believe world with all the sarcasm and jokes has rubbed off on me.

Each character I look up to be, becomes a part of me. I started recognizing the personalities of the characters I admire in myself. (I mainly watched comedy sitcoms)

I began watching the sitcom called F.R.I.E.N.D.S. My parents didn't stop me from binge watching the series as they felt that I needed to laugh more (plus they liked to watch it as well).

I started to identify strongly with the character Chandler Bing from F.R.I.E.N.D.S. I, like Chandler Bing, have a security blanket and this made me relate to him. I started connecting my characteristics with him and started to use his sarcastic humour. His sarcasm appealed to me. It was rather interesting, and I felt that I could actually pull off having a similar sense of humour.

It was simple to hide everything with jokes and snide remarks. Everyone accepted that as normal. Surprisingly, with all these 'jokes', I was known as the cool kid, which amazed me.

It appeared to be genuine; I had given the impression that I was laid back and funny. What they interpreted as jokes was just me giving out rude comments and snarky comebacks.

It finally became a part of who I was.

I've always struggled dealing with emotions; I'm not great at figuring out my emotions to be honest, so I end up acting before thinking things through.

And trust me, when I act on something, we all know nothing good will come out of it. I prefer to think of myself as a complex person, largely because I feel no one understands me, and it's commonly known that I'm not the one to express and let them know how I was feeling.

Then came possibly the most annoying phase ever (according to my parents)... the one with the mood swings.

I couldn't process my own emotions. My already existing anger problems became worse, and I had added some extra seasoning to the already over-spiced dish.

Chapter 6

Lacuna

Hollowness, blackness, despair

Plummeting into a haze

Hopeless as it be

Holding on to tears...

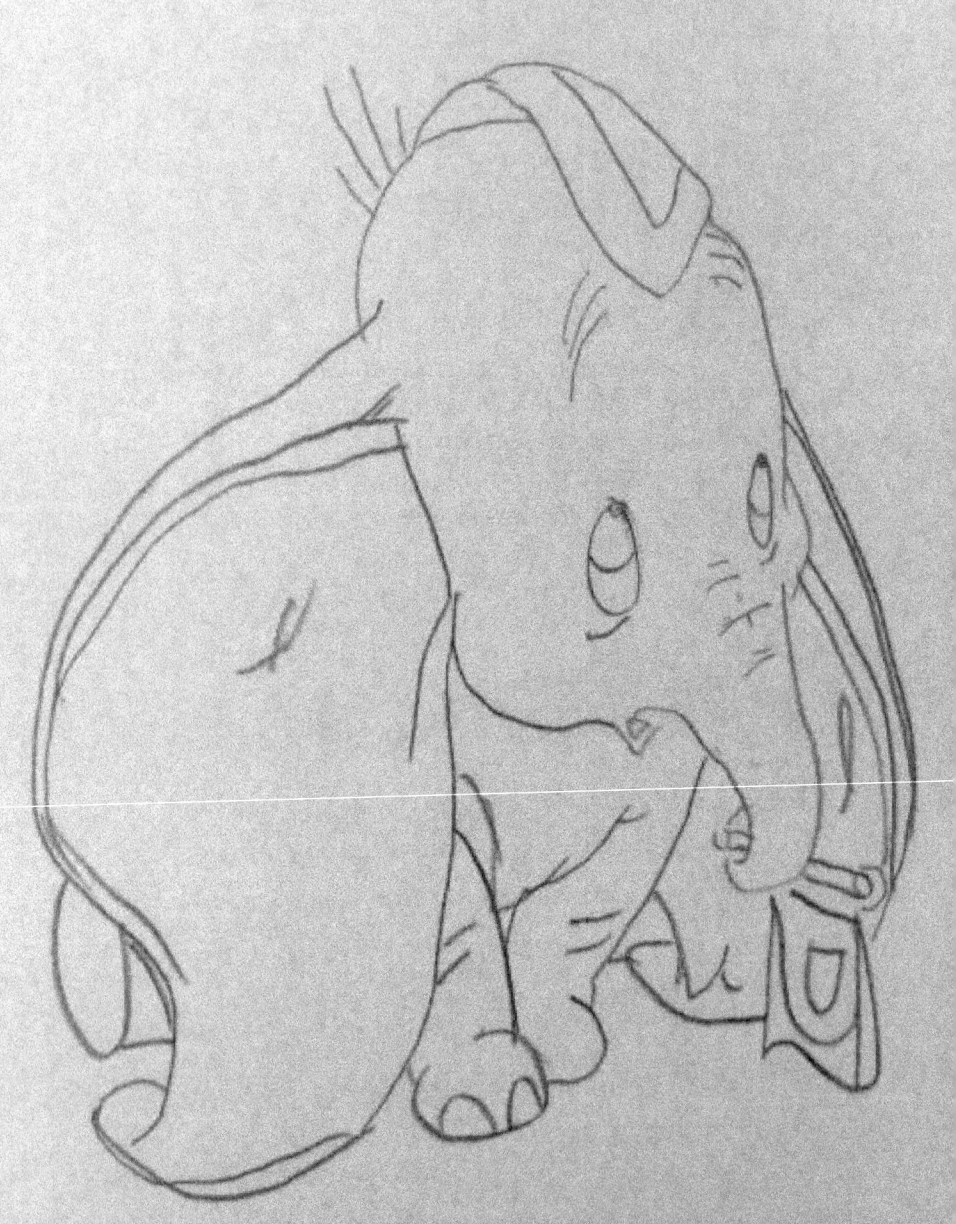

My mind was like a palimpsest. I started rethinking everything and was sceptical of everything I knew about myself.

I was completely lost. I felt like a completely different person, as if I had never known my thinking of myself in various perspectives. I really wanted to figure out myself (like an old person). Mostly I wanted to know who I was. I constantly started pondering about my birth parents. I was engulfed with curiosity and felt like I needed answers. My mind was always occupied with thoughts about my birth. I felt as if my glass was half full.

I didn't really know anything about my birth family. So, did I have siblings or even step siblings? Whenever I danced and was appreciated by others for being a natural born dancer, I tried to relate it to my birth parents wondering if I had got these genes from them. I started to link almost everything to my birth parents. My main focus was my looks (I know I look fantastic!). Whenever my friends would discuss certain features of their face resembling their parents, my heart would yearn to have some information about them so that I too could say that I have eyes like my birth mom or smile like my birth dad.

I confess that this phase was just about me trying to connect to the people I didn't know, which as vague as it sounds was equally painful. But the uncanny resemblance that I share with my Father, somehow stuck a bandage on my open wound.

There was nothing much I could do about this aspect of my life. Being the overdramatic person that I am, I decided, it was best to ignore any talks or thoughts about adoption. I guess this too did not help. As I was suppressing all these feelings, I realised that I was turning into this angry little *Shrek*. I was irritated at the slightest provocation and I started snapping at everyone in my life.

I wasn't able to connect to anyone and I slowly started to withdraw from people. I felt rather insecure about who I was. If I didn't know everything about me, I felt like I couldn't be sure or confident. *"This anxiety helped a lot when it came to not understanding people."* I had no self-confidence and had trust issues as well as major abandonment issues. This led to shying away from any opportunity possible. I thought this was who I was.

As I have mentioned earlier, I was a really fussy child and I always demanded to get what I wanted, and I also never used to give in to persuasive attempts. I was adamant. I was a firecracker waiting to be lit up. I used to throw tantrums and had my own way of getting what I wanted from my parents. This equation somehow changed after I was told that I was adopted. I just felt the old me slip away, slowly fading. I felt like I needed to please my parents at all costs because I was scared that they would send me back to the orphanage. Stupid thing to think? Yes. But as I said I had major trust issues and these abandonment issues were pulling me into this dark gloomy void.

Along with my self-confidence, my self-esteem had shot down a lot. I, then, developed a severe case of panic attacks. I started to feel my dyslexia resurface as I wasn't able to understand anything once again. The words and the numbers again didn't make any sense. This affected my studies and grades. I wasn't able to concentrate and I could not do well in subjects. This fear not only impacted my studies but also my tennis. I was on a losing streak which had affected me big time. I was against playing any sort of tournaments or matches. This fear of losing impacted my ranking majorly. My ranking shot down quicker than it had gone up. I started to develop a phobia. This phobia put me in a scenario where I was fighting against a shark, with no chance of survival, the saddest part being that the shark was just a figment of my imagination.

After some time, I realised that harping on this topic or even trying to ignore it wasn't helping me. So, I made many attempts to move on and accept my past. I tried to talk about it with people to get used to being known as adopted, not for others but for myself.

I knew whatever happens this would always be a part of my life.

Chapter 7

Burgeon

Only beginning to flourish

From all the struggles

And stings which may as well be a bee

I changed ….

Or at least I began to do so

To overcome tacenda,

To finally be me…

As a couple of years went by, after the life changing disclosure that I was adopted, my life reactions were to dig myself a dark hole and subsist in it with a bowl full of despondency. I, in a way, made agony my motive. I was rather disheartened thinking about where I was headed.

I wanted to get rid of who I was and change into someone new. In a way, I did change. You gotta hand it to me...I was a child. Because, at this point, I was imagining a change in the lines of where a donkey turned to a horse. It was rather unrealistic. I should've wanted to be a caterpillar who burgeoned into the butterfly that came out of a cocoon.

I then decided that to get rid of my problems I should find the root cause and get rid of it. My problems centred around me being an adopted child. Getting rid of me meant shutting myself out to forget that I was adopted. I wanted to live my life as a child, not as an adopted child or the birth child.

I thought forgetting about everything would be a fool proof plan as only my family mattered, and I knew that there was a rare chance they would talk about this to me. This was the stupidest thing I had ever done and I have done *a lot* of stupid things. Obviously, this plan wasn't fool proof as I was the one who wanted to discuss this more in depth but was not able to bring myself to do it.

Forgetting is never an option.

Instead of being insecure about this topic I tried to face it, instead of running away from it, I slowly tried to face the facts, which piqued my curiosity in myself. There was no point in starting out with a clean slate. Instead, I decided to add on to who I am.

To begin with, I didn't want a transformation. I wanted a change.

I figured, if I changed my style it would do. I started experimenting by dyeing my hair in different colours. If one day I was a blue Macaw, the next time I would be a red parrot. Though it did raise a few eyebrows and potential trouble in school, it did nothing to lighten the existing problems. So, as a typical teenager I resorted to clothes. I went from short shorts phase to full on torn jeans phase (which my Father could not digest). Next step was to find my mental peace, which was, in my opinion, to replace it with whatever materialistic item I could find online (something that irked my Mother).

By the end of this phase I thought I was OK with the fact that I was adopted. I focused on how tough it must've been for my birth Mother to give up her child so that the child could have a better future, one which she could not provide. It would have taken so much strength to do this. That thought helped find some peace with the fact that I was adopted. This also encouraged me to bond with my parents after this troublesome phase where I felt I had distanced myself from them.

Instead of deciding to remain miserable while doing nothing, I gradually realised that I could have redirected my anger and sadness into something helpful, which could have changed my vibe to only positivity. I had missed out on so many chances/opportunities because of me wallowing in a pool of self-pity, which I started to regret massively. I knew that I had to do something about it.

This eventually happened. It was fate that allowed me to seize an opportunity to better myself.

One day during family dinner, the conversation deviated to a picture of my Grandfather, with Field Marshal Sam Manekshaw receiving an award for his dissertation during his serving days. My Grandfather went on to discuss Psychology with me and how he had done a case study on his friend who had succumbed to alcoholism. This branch of Psychology intrigued me.

On further talks with my grandpa, I realised that this Psychoanalytical theory – Transactional Analysis, could help me better myself, seize what I have lost and create a beginning for a different aspect of my life, one, which would help me blossom into something rather fantastic and could help me in future too.

Thus started my actual journey into this new world.

PART -III

FORE SEE, FORE COME

Chapter 8
Introduction to TA

Transactional Analysis is a famous and very successful psychological theory created in the 1970s by the late Dr. Eric Berne.

Transactional Analysis raises your consciousness while elevating your thinking, allowing you to understand your own challenging and dysfunctional behaviours and communication patterns in a better way, allowing you to form deeper connections with yourself and the environment.

The Ego States or the PAC (Parent, Adult, Child) concept is the foundation of Transactional Analysis.

Parent, Adult, and Child (PAC) are the three ego states.

Parent:

The attitudes and behaviours that are seen and copied from the individual's caregivers and models make up the parent ego state. As an adult, a person in this Ego-State may be very critical, judgemental, often making decisions for others, protective, caring, and so on.

Adult:

The Adult Ego State appears in a child at the age of six months and is primarily concerned with assessing facts, reasoning, thinking, analysing and responding to available data. Many Transactional Analysis writers compare it to a computer, which is exclusively concerned with reason and logic.

When a person is in the Adult Ego-State, he or she acts in ways that are directly connected to the present moment. Without being affected by any other Ego-State, the individual is free to select their reaction. He or she will seek answers in the most efficient and reasonable manner possible, while remaining emotionally detached from the problem.

A person in the Adult Ego-State is generally direct in their approach, is engaged in the dialogue without being judgemental, and understands how to use reasoning in opposing circumstances.

Child:

While being impacted by their ideas as replayed in childhood, a person in this Ego-State shows behaviours, feelings, or may ponder about circumstances. Attitude is determined by emotions triggered by previous behaviour.

Rebellion, joy, complaining, pouting, terror, anxiety, or even a lot of laughing may be displayed by someone in this Ego-State.

The Three Ego-States are never consciously recognised by a person. To ground their communication in the present circumstance, everyone re-experiences a part of the Parent Ego-State or the Child Ego-State.

Transactional analysis is a type of psychoanalysis that analyses social interactions and how we may enhance them.

Life positions are aspects of transactional analysis. Our ego states, or the ways we think, feel, and act are the foundations of transactional analysis. Our ego states are shaped by our interactions with our parents (Parent), past experiences as children (Child), and present settings (Adult).

Life positions are the fundamental ideas we have about ourselves and others that we use to explain our actions and decisions.

Our early experiences, up to the age of seven, determine our life positions which includes whether we regard ourselves and others as "OK" or "not OK." Being "OK" relates to feelings of goodness or worthiness; it is assumed that everyone comes into the world "OK."

Hippocrates proposed that personality traits and human behaviours are based on four distinct temperaments associated with four different bodily fluids ("humours"): **choleric** temperament (yellow bile from the liver), **melancholic** temperament (black bile from the kidneys), **sanguine** temperament (red bile from the kidneys) and **phlegmatic** temperament (red blood from the heart).

The imbalance of pairs led in one of four temperament groups (or personality types): **sanguine** (upbeat and social), **choleric** (irritable and short-tempered), **melancholy** (quiet and analytical), and **phlegmatic** (calm and collected) (being relaxed and peaceful).

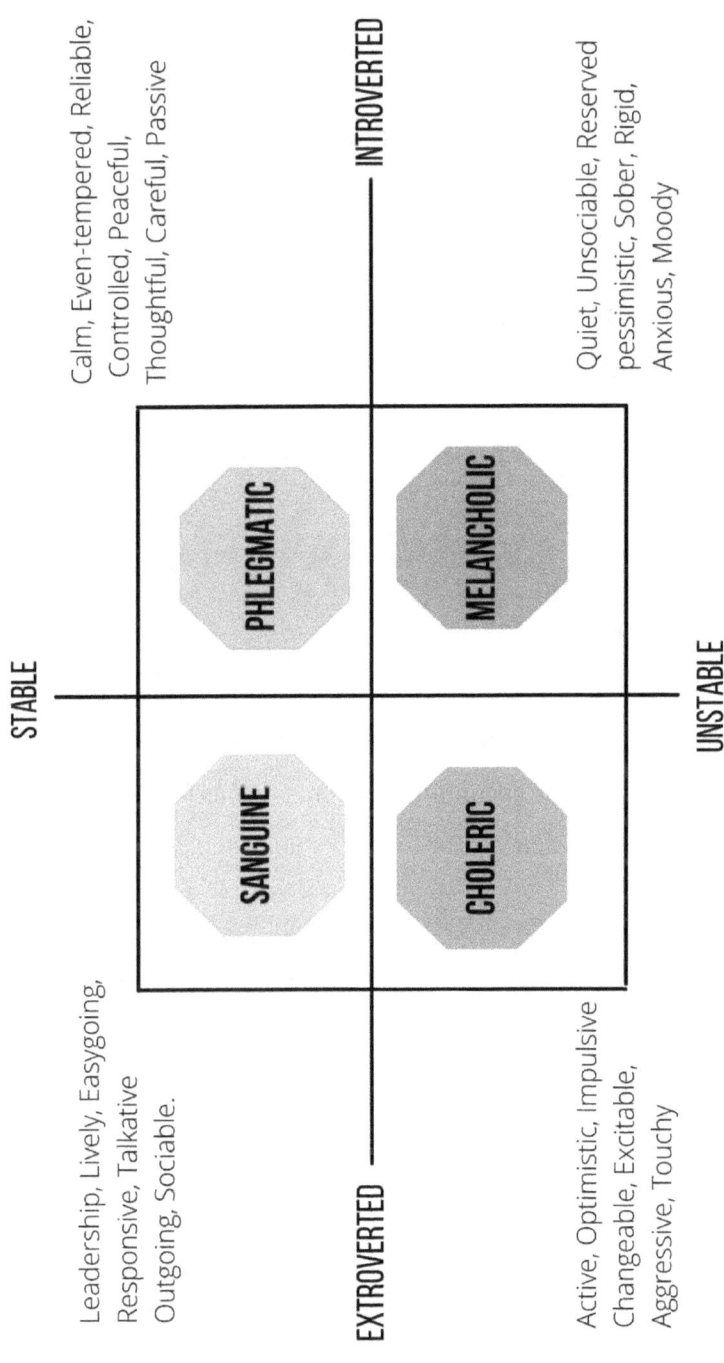

Dr. Eric Berne developed the notion of being "OK" to describe the classification of life situations which consisted of being fair to oneself and others, as well as viewing oneself and others as having equal rights.

The subjects of all positions, according to Berne, are focused on "I" against "Others," and their predicates are focused on being "OK" versus "not OK." As a result, the fundamental predicates are:

1. I am OK
2. I am not OK
3. You are OK
4. You are not OK

The I'm OK—You're OK position is regarded as the best, healthiest and most game-free position. Persons in this situation will believe that all people are intrinsically valued and deserving.

The phrase "people are OK" refers to their being or essence rather than their actions. This viewpoint is defined by an openness, honesty and trusting attitude. People who hold this attitude will work together and embrace themselves and others.

I'm OK - You're not OK is populated by individuals who project their problems onto others, blaming and criticising them.

A self-styled superior (the "I'm OK") projects wrath, contempt, or scorn onto a designated inferior or scapegoat (the "You're not OK") in transactional games that reinforce this position. In order to preserve a feeling of self as acceptable, this stance necessitates the presence of someone who is 'worse than.'

I'm not OK - You're OK stance is characterised by feelings of powerlessness and inadequacy in contrast to others. People in this position may overlook their own needs in favour of those of others, and they may see themselves as victims.

I'm not OK—You're not OK is a dismal, futile, and frustrating posture. Life appears boring and bleak from this vantage point. Self-destructive or aggressive behaviour may develop as a result of this.

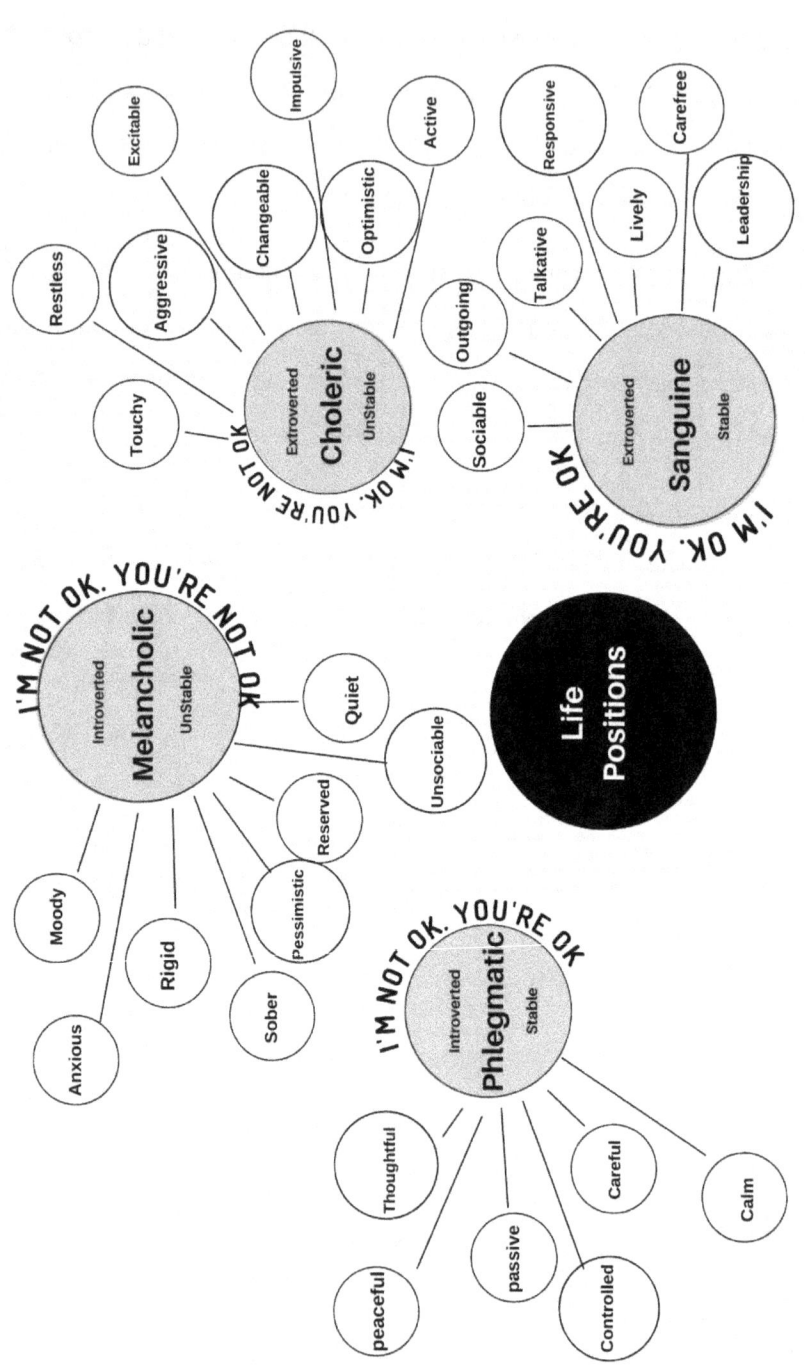

I had used the below questionnaire to analyse myself. This should help you all also to understand your temperament better. I do encourage you to use it to analyse yourself. It should be a' Yes/No' answer.

Personality Test : Hippocratic Scheme

(Adapted from "YOUR PERSONALITY," Geoffrey A Dudley BA PP 75 – 77)

Choleric

1. Do you tend to become easily excited?
2. Do you find it difficult to control your emotions?
3. Do you like to stick at a job until you have finished it?
4. When you plan something do you tackle it with enthusiasm?
5. If you felt strongly about some issue would you get up to speak about it at a public meeting?
6. Do you like to work quickly once you have started a task?
7. Have you ever made a serious mistake through acting without thinking?
8. Are you keenly ambitious to get on in life?
9. Are you inclined to worry?
10. Do you frequently lose your temper?

Sanguine

1. When things go well for you do you feel overjoyed?
2. When you hear a piece of good news do you want to tell all your friends about it?
3. When you undertake something new are you usually hopeful of succeeding it?
4. When you get worked up about a thing do you cool off fairly soon?
5. Do you usually manage to keep cheerful inspite of setbacks?
6. Have you ever been accused of being fickle?
7. Do you attach strong importance of good manners?
8. When you are fond of someone do you like to show your feelings openly?
9. Do other people find you a lively companion?
10. Are you capable of speaking openly without being unkind?

Phlegmatic

1. Do you tend to take a little interest in what is going around you?
2. Is it an effort for you to show affection for the members of your family?
3. Do you tend to take what you hear or read with a grain of salt?
4. Would you describe yourself as a pretty stolid sort of person?
5. Do you find it difficult to take sides over some controversial issue?
6. Do you believe in the proverb "Look before you Leap"?
7. Do you prefer to keep to yourself in company?
8. Do you remain calm in an emergency?
9. Do you dislike getting involved in an argument?
10. Do you find it hard to make conversation?

Melancholic

1. Are you liable to become easily depressed?

2. Are you apt to experience gloomy forebodings?

3. Do you find it difficult to make friends?

4. Do you prefer your own company to that of other people?

5. Are you shy about striking up a conversation with a stranger?

6. Are you reluctant to give up too easily when you encounter difficulties?

7. When someone asks you for your opinion do you hesitate to give it?

8. Do you get irritable at times?

9. Have you ever been complimented on your reliability?

10. When someone criticizes you, do you find it hard to think of a quick reply?

Chapter 9
Self-Analysis

Chapter 1:

The breakdown as an infant

Even though I didn't realise it until years later, I had inherited trauma. I was separated from my birth Mother at an early age because of which I experienced inherited trauma, which is practically an existing trauma.

It influences how I react to my surroundings. I believe this hereditary trauma manifested in the womb when a Mother had to go through the trauma of giving up her child for adoption and when I was missing out on the warmth of my birth Mother's embraces during the initial infant years and her breast milk.

During my stay in the orphanage, I was looked after by caretakers so I didn't always get the same attention as other new-borns who were with their birth Mother.

I was nurtured in an environment with many other children so I didn't have access to the usual nutritional food that other neonates received, nor the warmth.

To put it bluntly, I was touch deprived as a new-born child.

As I was an infant during this stage, I shall not do any psychoanalysis on myself.

Chapter 2 :

The Breakdown of : Under The Weather Forever

As the title recommends, I was always unwell. Though I never felt OK per say, I was Ok during the short intervals when I was healthy.

I was never able to play and enjoy childhood like the other children, not that I had an abnormal childhood or anything, I felt I had to sacrifice all that during the time that I was under the weather and be mature.

When I was sick, I also ended up thinking of what my parents would be going through. I had this impression created in my mind about everyone suffering around me and what problems it was creating. This didn't help my situation. I did try to be positive, but if I were to be honest, I wasn't completely Ok through this phase.

Based on the above analysis, I was in a controlled and passive mindset. My temperament was phlegmatic and so I was in the life positioning of 'I AM NOT OK YOU ARE OK'.

Temperament - Phlegmatic

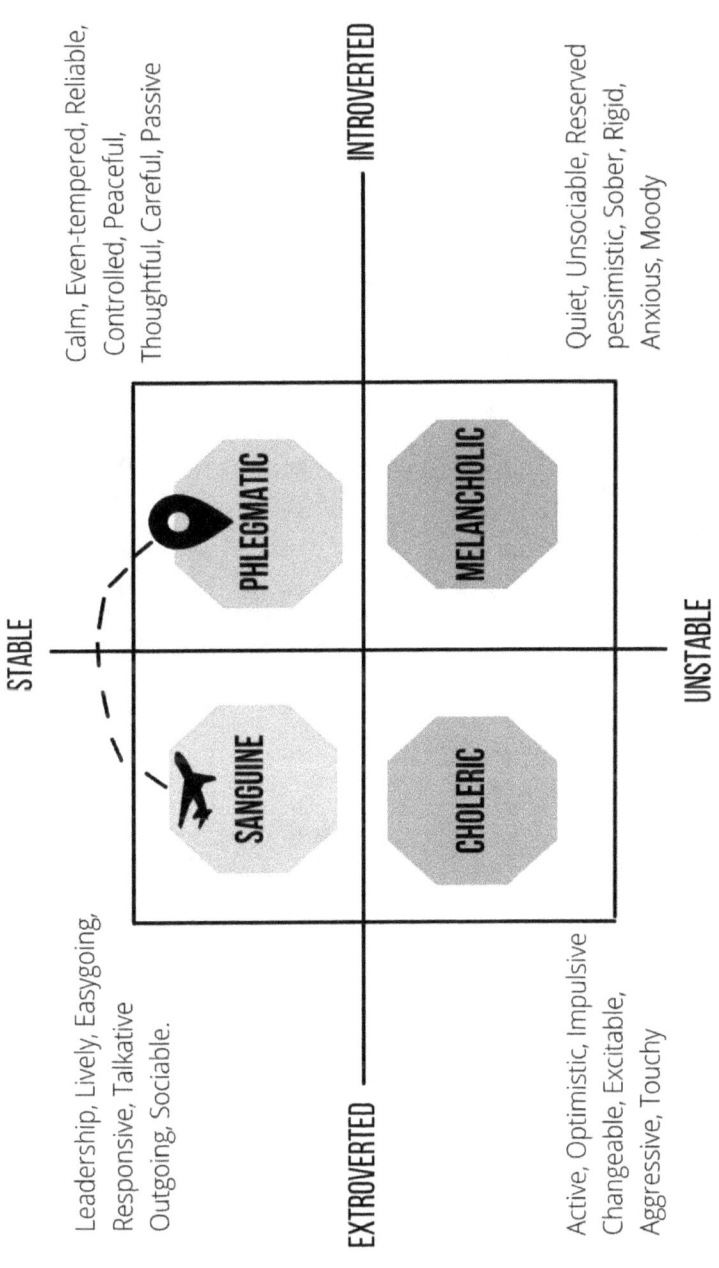

83

Life-positioning- I AM NOT OK YOU ARE OK

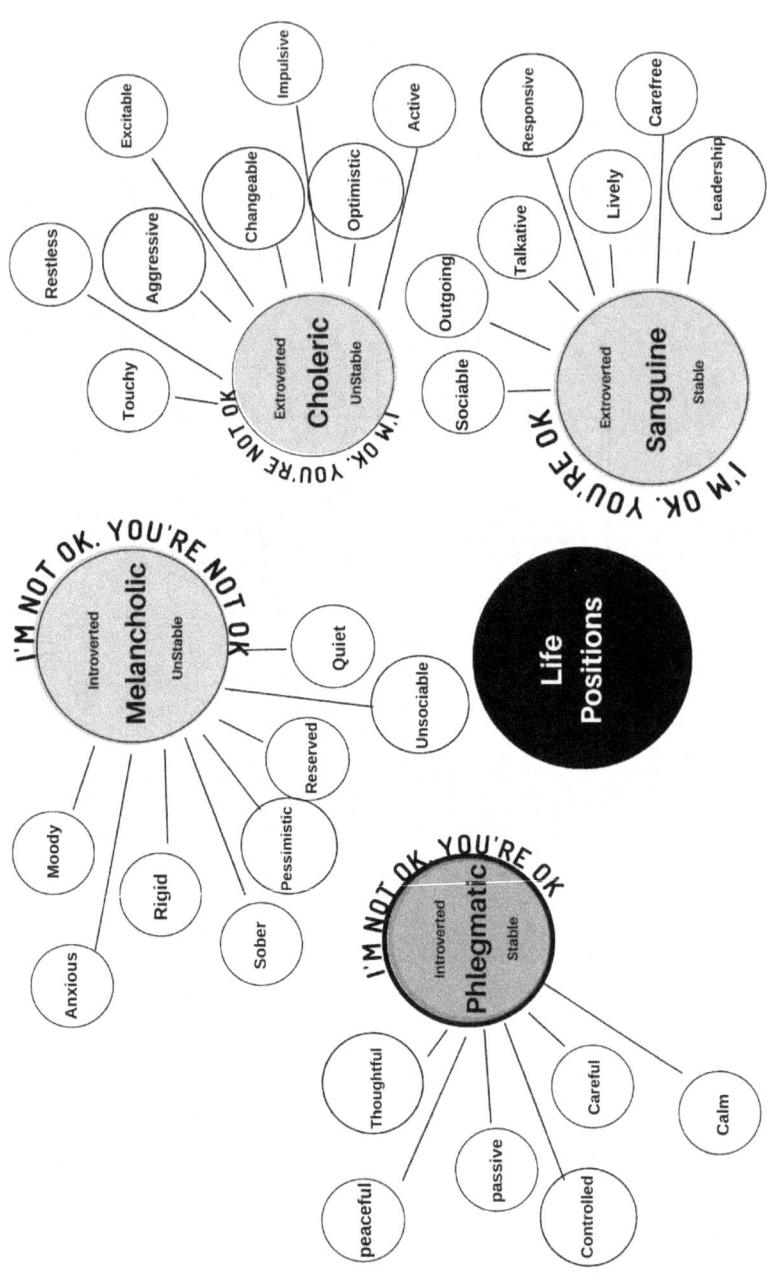

Chapter 3:

The breakdown of : Jab Hum Chotey Thei

As I have stated at the starting of this chapter, I have a security blanket. Having a security blanket could be due to issues such as insecurity, the fear of losing close ones, abandonment issues and separation anxiety. This blanket was my object constancy. I also had the symptoms of dyslexia.

In this chapter, looking back, I realise that I had low self-esteem which led me to have that "not OK' feeling.

I was rather stubborn, temperamental and had thrown a lot of temper tantrums. During this time, I was trying to assert the "I'm OK you're not Ok" feeling. Not accepting 'No' for my actions sending me into tantrums was just me asserting to change from "not OK" to "I am OK/ you're not OK."

I was attempting to change over from self "not OK" to "I am OK- you're not OK." The other prominent characteristic I had was that I tried to imitate boys by dressing up, acting and preferring their company. I felt like I didn't fit in and I wasn't attractive like how other girls are/were, this led me to go into the "I'm not OK" position.

Temperament - Phlegmatic

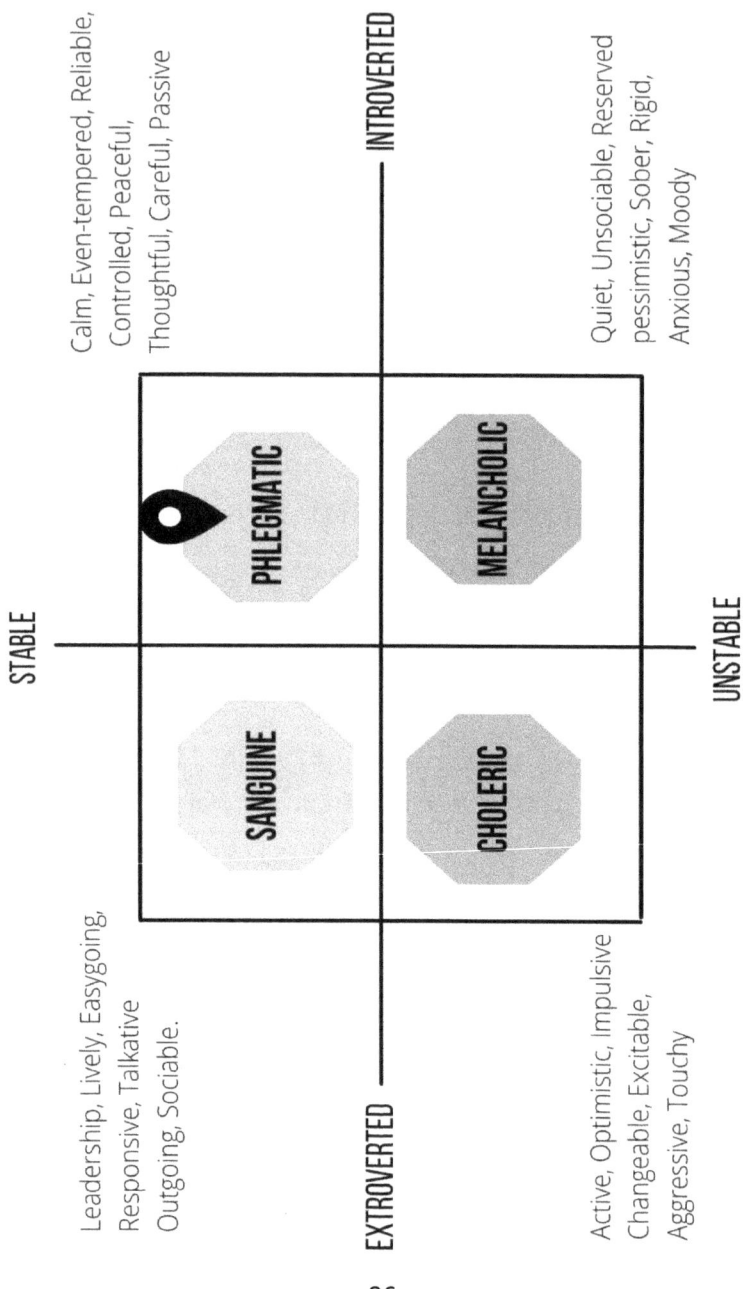

Life-positioning- I AM NOT OK YOU ARE OK

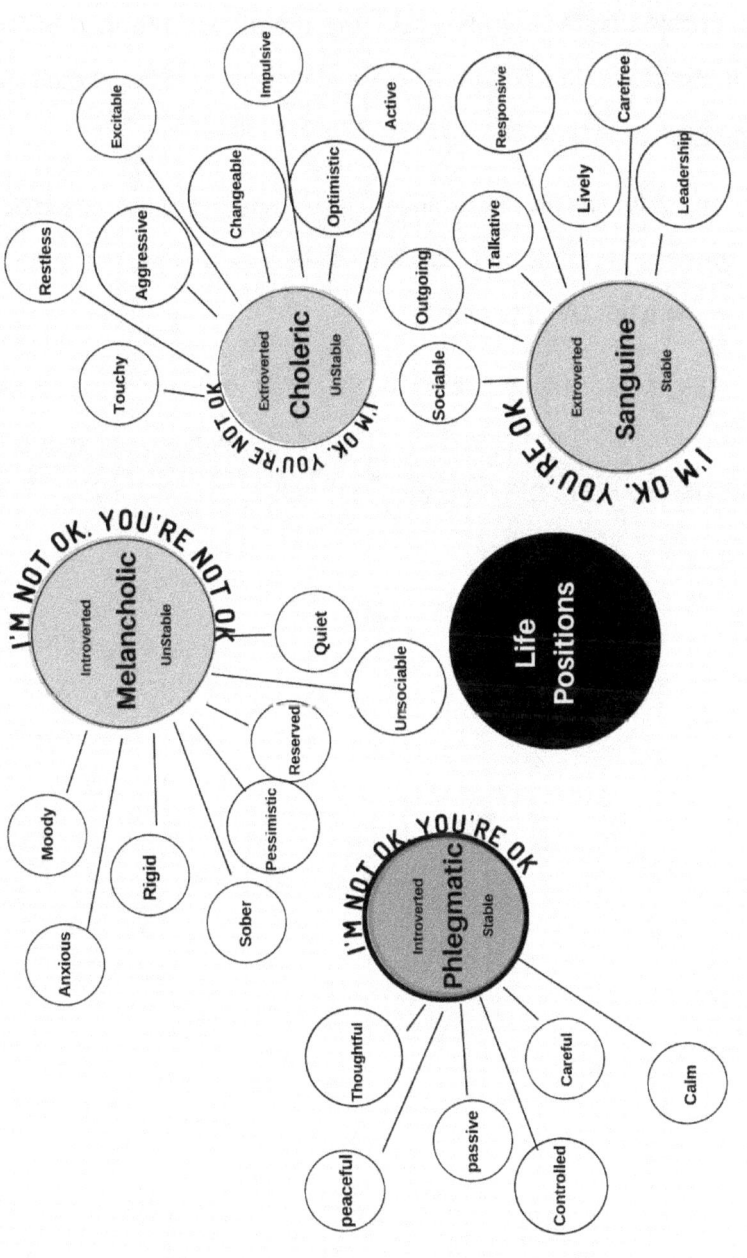

Breakdown of Chapter 4: Abrupt Disclosure

In this chapter I wrote about the time I was informed of being adopted. I was in a state of shock and disbelief when I learned that I had been adopted.

I was also sad and had a lingering curiosity regarding my biological Mother and that my parents were not biological ones. This put me in a "you are not OK" situation.

All I knew at the moment was that I felt my world was collapsing around me and nothing felt OK. I'd suddenly found myself in the "I'm not OK/you're not OK" life situation.

Temperament – Melancholic

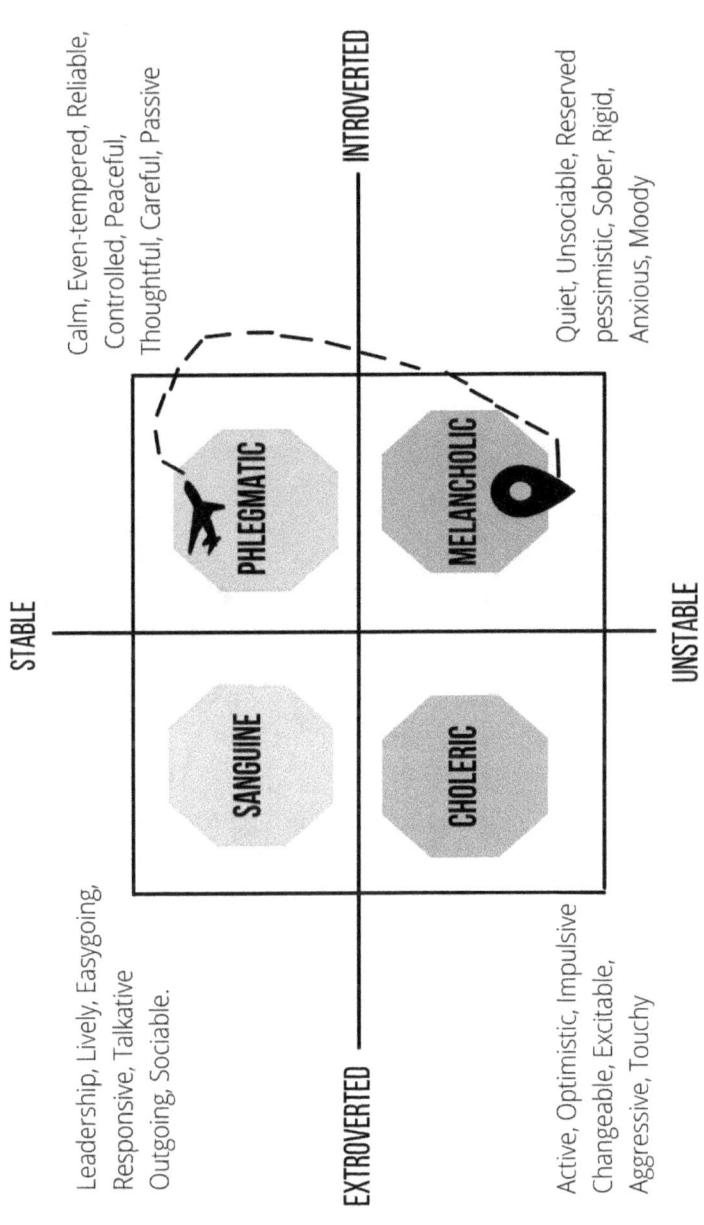

Life-positioning- I AM NOT OK YOU ARE NOT OK

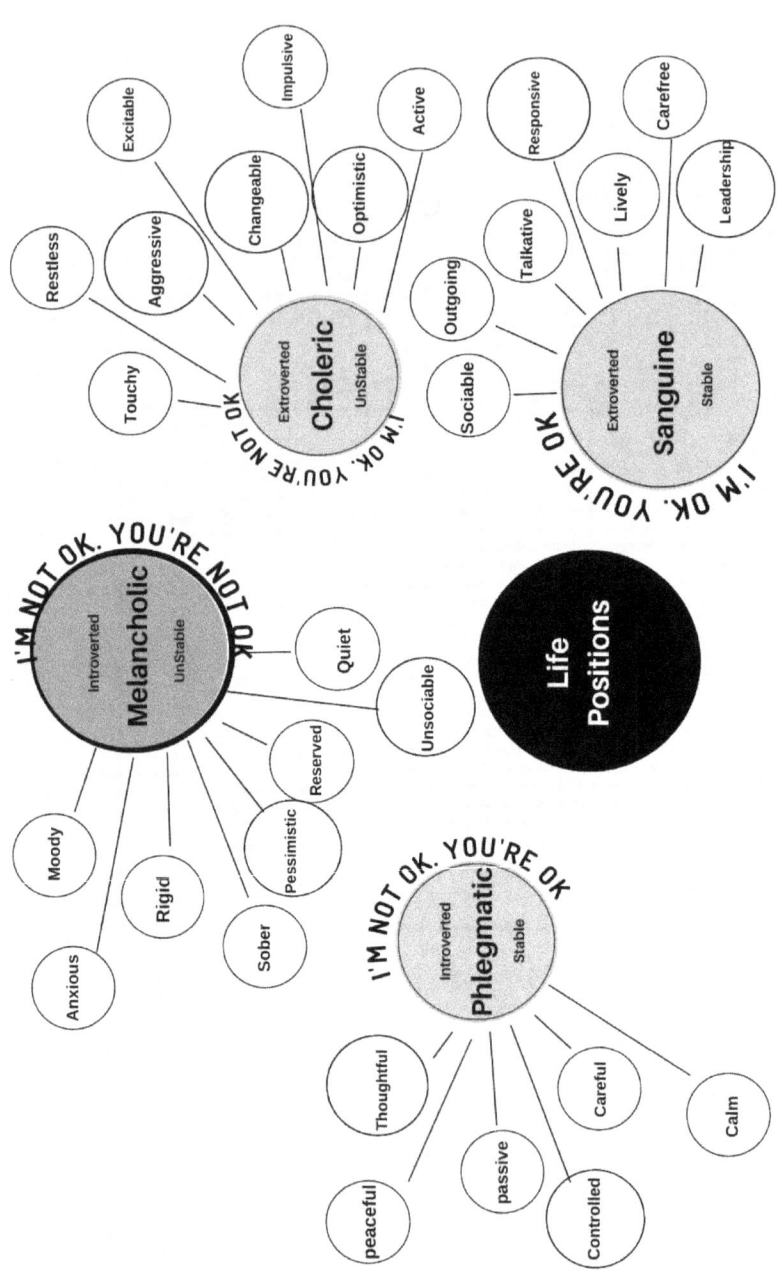

Breakdown of Chapter 5: That Sarcastic Kid

I had slipped into the "I'm not ok/you're not ok" trap in Chapter 4.

Throughout this chapter, I made a conscious effort to shift into the "I'm Ok/you're OK" mindset. By projecting sarcasm and proving to people that I am cool and being able to shut out the awful feeling of being an adopted child.

But my mind continued to be in the "I'm not ok/you're not ok" life positioning.

Temperament - Melancholic

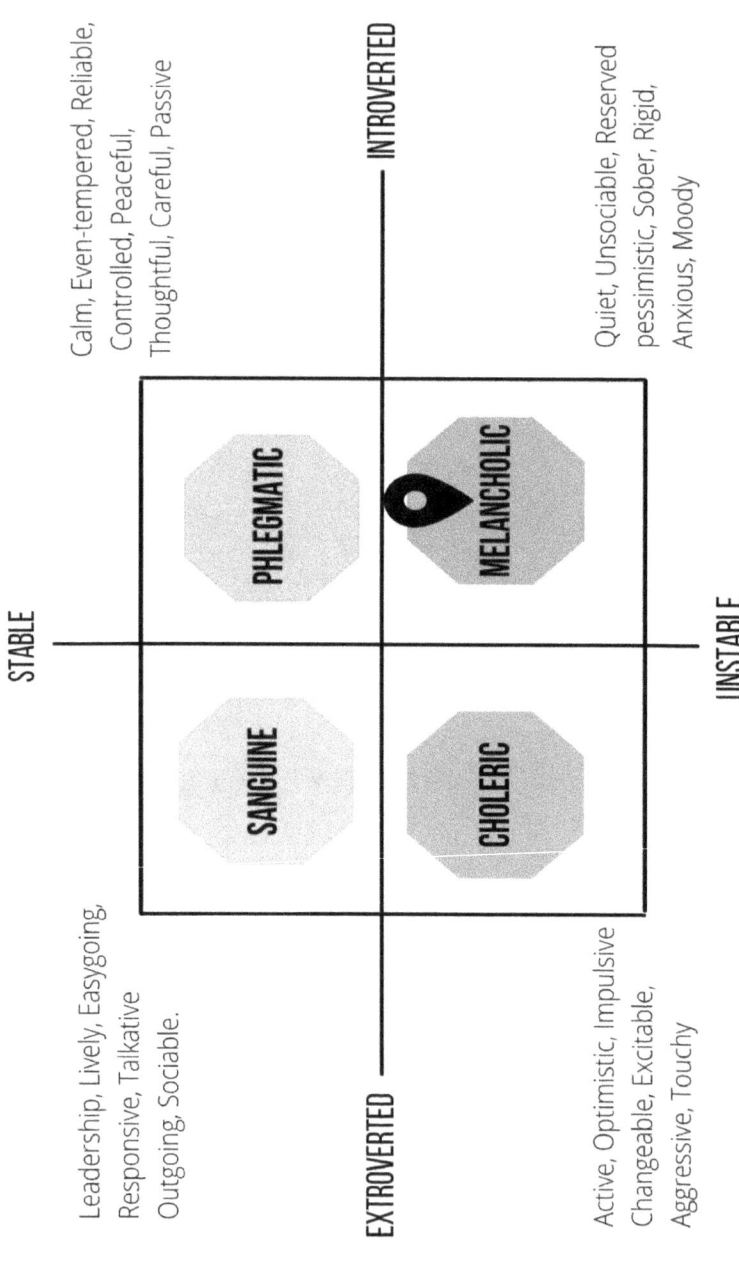

Life-positioning- I AM NOT OK YOU ARE NOT OK

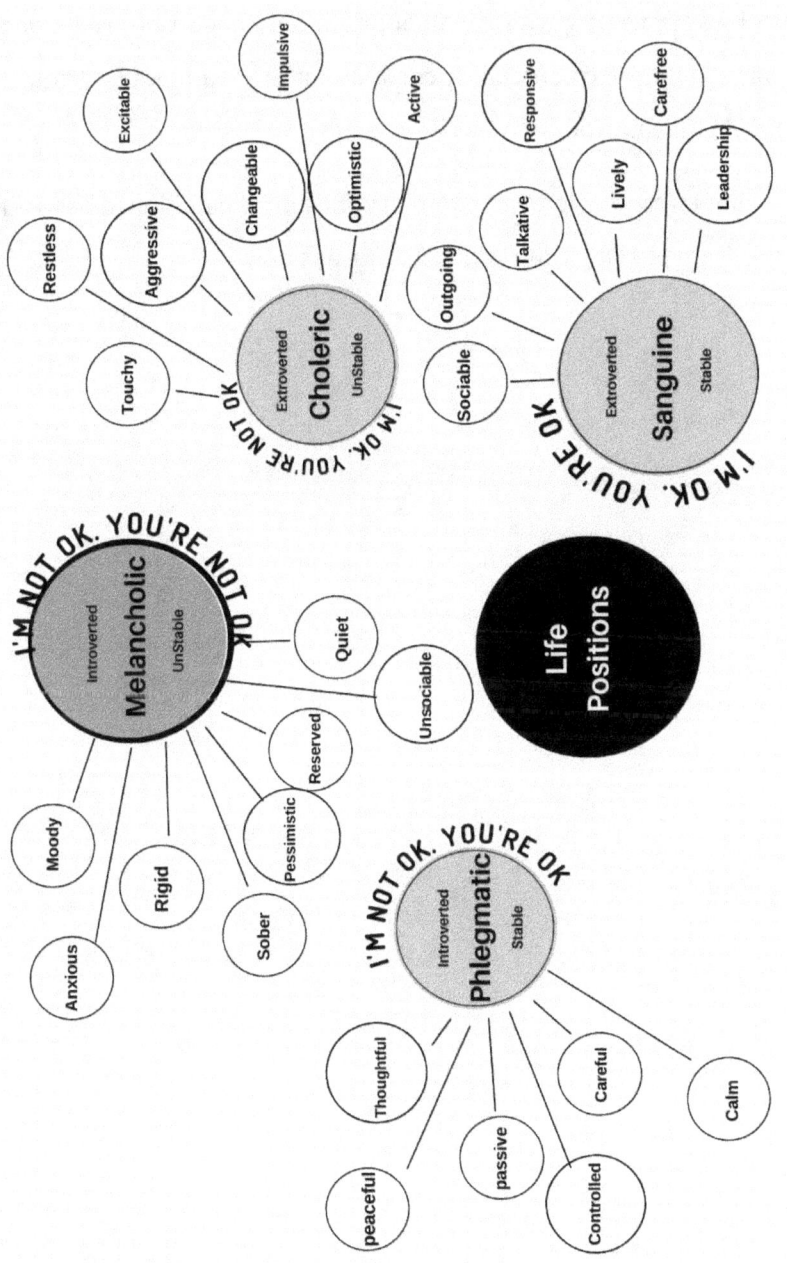

Breakdown of Chapter 6: Lacuna

I was struggling with my emotions in this chapter of my life and I was still trying to consciously come out of the "I am not OK/ You are not OK" life position.

But I wasn't able to as it kept haunting me. I had slipped deep into the "I am not OK/ You are not OK" life position.

Temperament - Melancholic

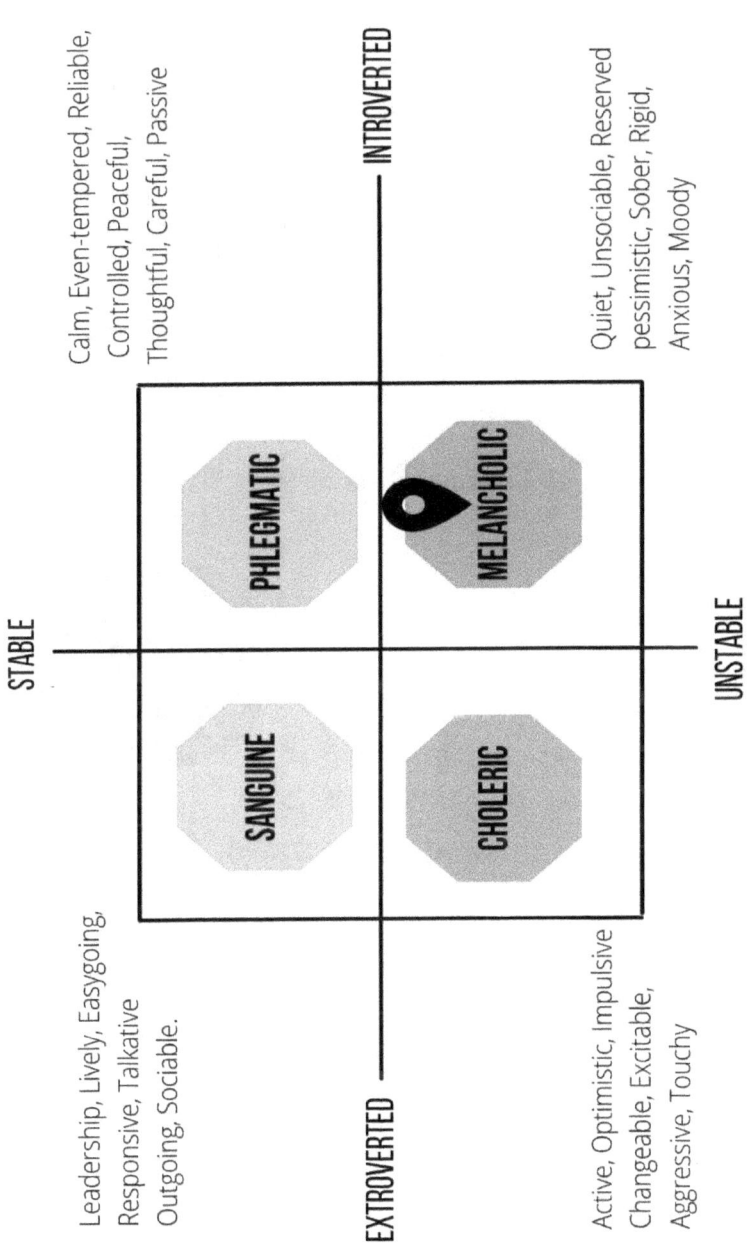

Life-positioning- I AM NOT OK YOU ARE NOT OK

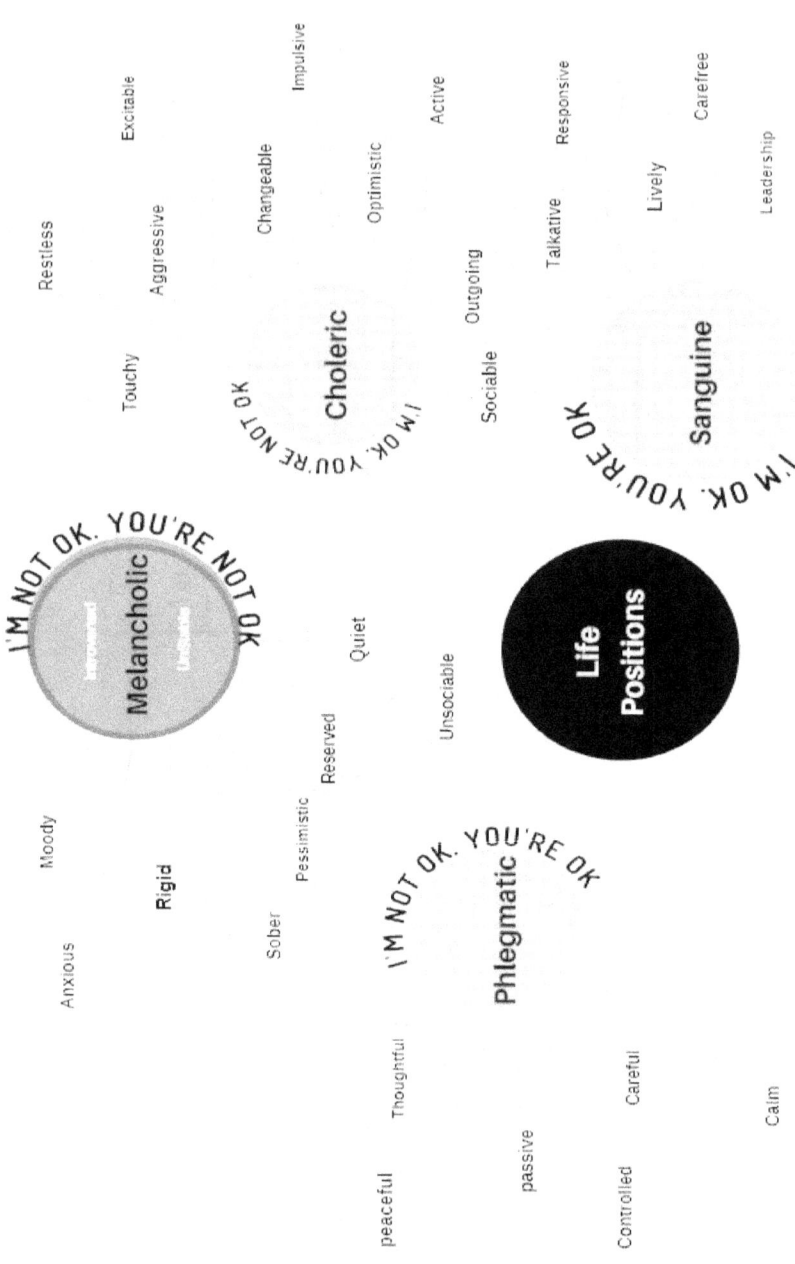

Breakdown of Chapter 7: Burgeon

I started making a conscious effort to adjust my mindset to "I'm OK/you're fine". The catalytic discussion about psychology based on TA with my Grandfather, and the attempt to make a real effort toward a positive change made a serious change.

I'm currently in the life position of "I'm Ok/You're not OK."

I shall give a detailed break up for this chapter and my future outlook.

Life-positioning- I AM OK YOU ARE NOT OK

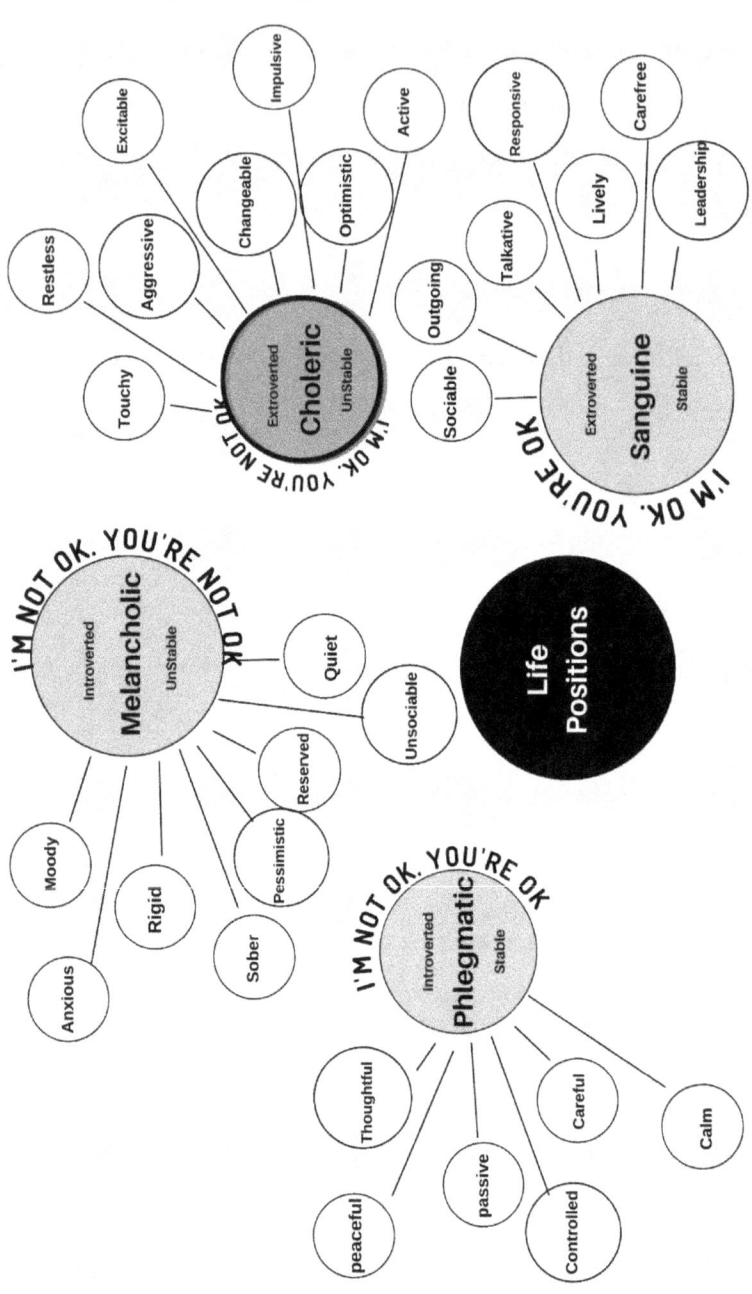

Some of the characteristics of this life positions are:

- Touchy
- Restless
- Aggressive
- Excitable
- Changeable
- Impulsive
- Optimistic
- Active

I have seen that I demonstrate all these characters and these characteristics are very prominent in me.

I'm trying to attain the ideal life position which is **"I'm OK/ you're OK'** and the characteristics of this life position.

The characteristics of this position are:

- Sociable
- Outgoing
- Talkative
- Responsive
- Lively

- Carefree

- Leadership

I have noticed that in the attempt to change my life position to "I'm OK/ you're OK', I have started to showcase some of these characteristics such as:

- Sociable

- Talkative

- Lively

In order to attain this life position, I would need to change a lot. In order to do that I will need to focus on a couple of characteristics I already have dominant in me.

Touchy: By striving to keep silent, I can modify this character. For example, not replying to every comment, criticism or action. Recognize that maximising unpleasant feelings takes time and effort, when you're dealing with a strong emotion, it isn't always like this. When I start to overreact, instead of directing my attention and concentration inward, I keep my focus on what's going on around me.

Remember that being sensitive is a wonderful thing since it implies that you're sympathetic and understanding of other people's circumstances. Mine is just a smidgeon above the average, bordering on hypersensitivity.

Some of the characteristics of this life positions are:

- Touchy
- Restless
- Aggressive
- Excitable
- Changeable
- Impulsive
- Optimistic
- Active

I have seen that I demonstrate all these characters and these characteristics are very prominent in me.

I'm trying to attain the ideal life position which is **"I'm OK/ you're OK'** and the characteristics of this life position.

The characteristics of this position are:

- Sociable
- Outgoing
- Talkative
- Responsive
- Lively

- Carefree
- Leadership

I have noticed that in the attempt to change my life position to "I'm OK/ you're OK', I have started to showcase some of these characteristics such as:

- Sociable
- Talkative
- Lively

In order to attain this life position, I would need to change a lot. In order to do that I will need to focus on a couple of characteristics I already have dominant in me.

Touchy: By striving to keep silent, I can modify this character. For example, not replying to every comment, criticism or action. Recognize that maximising unpleasant feelings takes time and effort, when you're dealing with a strong emotion, it isn't always like this. When I start to overreact, instead of directing my attention and concentration inward, I keep my focus on what's going on around me.

Remember that being sensitive is a wonderful thing since it implies that you're sympathetic and understanding of other people's circumstances. Mine is just a smidgeon above the average, bordering on hypersensitivity.

This can have a negative impact on my mental health, particularly if you take things too personally and linger on them for an extended amount of time. However, before I start berating myself for being a cry-baby or a whiner, I should take a deep breath and stop. Concentrating on negative labels will simply draw attention to these characteristics which can be troublesome. Instead, I should fill my mind with happy thoughts.

Restless: Meditation offers several benefits and it's powerful enough to regulate the stress response in the body. Practicing meditation every day can help you live in the present moment. I'll be able to separate myself from feelings of restlessness and anxiety and return to a peaceful state.

There are options to practice meditation, on our own or we could join a group meditation session. It's important to make meditation a part of our daily practice, the more we work at it, the better we'll get at managing our feelings.

During a period of restlessness, taking a few deep breaths might help our body and mind to relax. It triggers our parasympathetic nervous system and forces us to take in more oxygen. Deep breathing should be practised for at least 10 minutes each day, with the goal of increasing to half an hour. When we're in a stressful position and need to de-stress fast, taking a step back and taking a few deep breaths will help.

Aggressive: It may be beneficial to speak with someone about situations that make you feel aggressive. Consulting a psychologist has definitely helped me control my aggressiveness to a great extent. In some cases, adopting changes to our lifestyle can help us avoid frustrating situations.

We can also come up with ways to deal with frustrating situations, like delaying response time, counting to 10 before acting on a situation. We can learn to communicate more openly and honestly without being hostile.

Excitable: I definitely need to seek out signals that alert me of my over-excitement. When over excited, one may be more outspoken, confrontational and demanding, and may lack a sense of stability. It's also possible that you'll become disoriented about your surroundings. Meditation will assist you in de-stressing. Move around while listening to music, looking at different colours, eating something or drinking water. It is necessary to teach the mind to not oscillate between highs and lows. This process can be aided by taking a detached approach to our emotions, viewing them objectively and without judgement.

Impulsive: To have a better control on our impulses we should spend some time talking to ourselves or others who are involved with us. Declaring your method aloud can assist you in identifying areas where you could improve your thinking. When we're in a stressful situation, having an impartial opinion might help us avoid making assumptions and making rash decisions. Consider circumstances when you don't jump to conclusions and instead take your time. What was it that kept you from making snap decisions? What was the point of waiting? What did you gain from the time you spent waiting?

The bottom line is to investigate and activate our innate curiosity. Think about what more is there to explore the next time we're about to jump to a conclusion or make a hasty decision. First, inquire as to why we believe the circumstance or problem is occurring, and then inquire as to why we believe that is occurring. Then ask it once more. We'll have studied other data that might lead us to a different decision on how to proceed by the time you've dug down five times on what you thought the original conclusion was.

These emotions are very tough to understand and change. But with time I will learn to have a better control over them. I am sure these slight changes in my lifestyle will bring in major changes in my behaviour and attitude towards life.

I know I will slip back from time to time, but as long as I have this narrative to go back to, I will be able to analyse my situation better and act on it consciously.

As long as I am positively working on changing a few areas of my life, I am confident that I will soon one day be in the life positioning of "I'm Ok/You're OK."

Ideal Temperament - Sanguine

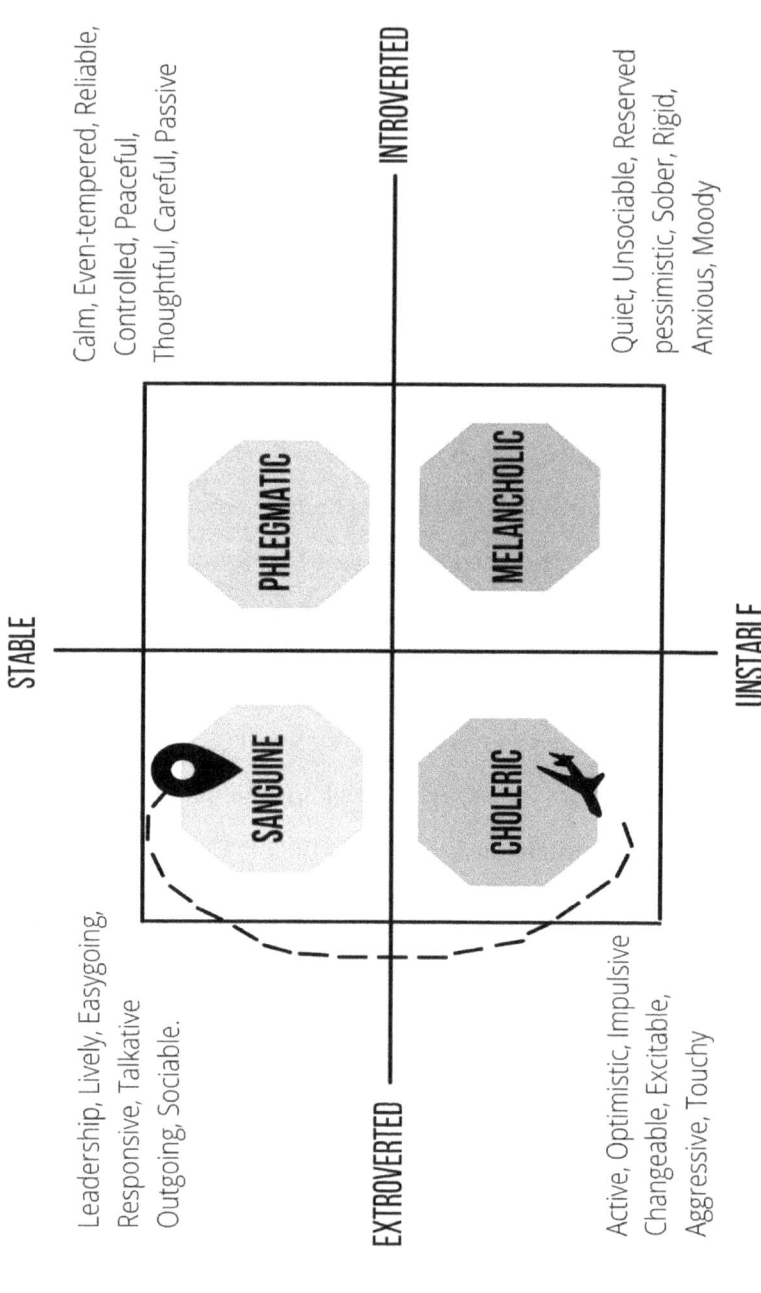

Ideal Life-positioning- I AM OK YOU ARE OK

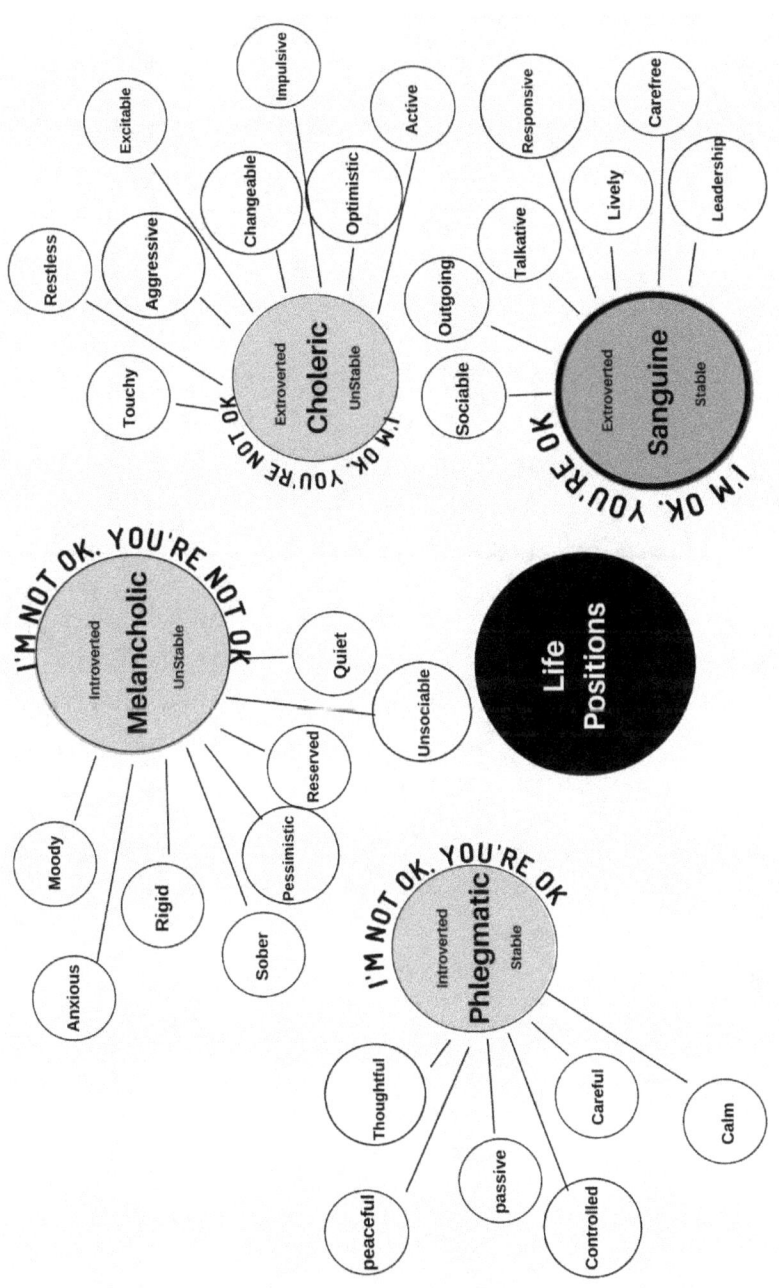

Epilogue

I don't know what my future consists of. But I can say that I'm grateful for having this narrative to look back on.

My interactions with my family and friends while researching for this book was nostalgic and enjoyable. My parents had documented my life in an orderly manner which helped me an easy access to go through my adoption papers, pictures stored month wise and all my medical history which was neatly filed. I hope to grow up to be as organised as they were.

By writing down my thoughts and feelings which were tormenting me, which for sure was not so easy to write, I realised I was hiding behind an invisible veil, looking at the world and people with a hazy outlook. This journey has helped me to rethink and evaluate my life until now. This book has helped me understand my attitude amongst other things. I now know which traits or characteristics I need to cultivate for a positive clearer outlook.

There will be a lot of changes in the future. It's inevitable.

I would like to encourage any teenager, adopted or not, to write their narrative to understand the value of the good things that have happened in our lives and to look beyond our present woes.

We all gain knowledge from our experiences. Seeking knowledge from another's perspective as an input of their experiences, will help fulfil the need of adopting parents, birth parents, and adoptees to an extent.

To use this as an opportunity to share my adoption journey and perspective, as well as, to open a window for adoptive and foster families showcasing a variety of adoptee's perspectives. A small step from my end desired to assist adoptees and foster children to thrive in life despite their trauma.

Each element of the adoption triad has its own set of safeguards that might operate as barriers to transparency in homes and families. I hope this narrative helps families who know not all of their children's emotional needs, and so have been looking for post-adoption help in the form of workshops and communities.

This journal will also be useful to me in the future.

I can't anticipate the future; I can only influence it to a certain extent. It may go in either direction. But I have this book to go to, and it will always assist me.

About The Author

Vritika Rene Viswanathan, born in 2007, resides in Coimbatore, the cotton city of Tamil Nadu in India. She is an ardent tennis player and has been playing since the age of six. She has a flair in writing poetry and sketches to unwind.

This book was born as a result of her school project. As she narrated her journey as an adopted child and as she researched more on the troubles faced by children in similar situations, she was encouraged to reach out with her perspective to live a life positively and to look beyond present woes.

Thus, penned her first book "Much More than Love".

Bibliography

- "Adopted Children Often Face Mental Health Struggles as Young Adults." Claudia Black Center, 2 Aug. 2021, www.claudiablackcenter.com/adopted-children-often-face-mental-health-struggles-as-young-adults/.

- "Color Your Own Deadpool (Trade Paperback)." Marvel, https://www.marvel.com/comics/collection/56817/color_your_own_deadpool_trade_paperback.

- Eric Berne MD
  A layman's Guide to Psychiatry and Psycho Analysis - Cox & Hyman Ltd, London, 1978

- Geoffrey A Dudley
  Your personality and have to use it: Bombay, Jaico Publishing House, 1970

- HJ Eysenek, Glenn Wilson
  Know your own personality – Pelican Books, 1976

- Long-Term Issues for the Adopted Child." Mental Help Long-term Issues for the Adopted Child Comments, www.mentalhelp.net/parenting/long-term-issues-for-the-adopted-child/.

- "Understanding the Relationship between Adoption & Mental Health Issues." Vertava Health Massachusetts, 26 Apr. 2021, vertavahealthmassachusetts.com/adoption-mental-health-issues/.

- Murray, Heather. "Transactional Analysis - Eric Berne." Transactional Analysis - Eric Berne | Simply Psychology, 25 Jan. 2021, https://www.simplypsychology.org/transactional-analysis-eric-berne.html.

- Muriel James & Dorothy Jongeward –
  Born to win: Transactional analysis with Gestalt Experiments, Philippines, Addison – Weasly Publishing Co-ine, 1971

- "Nephrotic Syndrome." Mayo Clinic, Mayo Foundation for Medical Education and Research, 30 Jan. 2020, https://www.mayoclinic.org/diseases-conditions/nephrotic-syndrome/symptoms-causes/syc-20375608#:~:text=Nephrotic syndrome is a kidney ailment, excess water from your blood.

- "22 Cartoon Coloring Pages Ideas in 2021: Cartoon Coloring Pages, Coloring Books, Coloring Pages." Pinterest, 25 Jan. 2021, https://in.pinterest.com/heatherjwhite77/cartoon-coloring-pagea/.

- Robinson, Tasha. "Can Science Fiction Map a Positive Future?" Polygon, Polygon, 15 Oct. 2020, https://www.polygon.com/2020/10/15/21515901/science-fiction-dystopia-utopia-stories.

- Robert Frager & James Fadiman
  Personality and Personal growth – New York, Harper & Row Publishers, 1984

- shadowline2000. Original Production Animation Drawing of Dumbo from "Dumbo," 1941, 1 Jan. 1970, http://greganimationart.blogspot.com/2019/01/original-production-animation-drawing_11.html.

- Thomas A Harris, MD
  I'm OK- You're OK: Transactional Analysis, New Delhi Sterling Publishers (p) Ltd, 1970

- "What Is Transactional Analysis Theory?" The Affinity Centre, 4Jan2021, https://affinitycentre.co.uk/transactional-analysis-theory-explained/.

- William Redd, PHD and William Sleator
  Take Charge – Random House, inc, New York, 1978

You Write. We Publish.

To publish your own book, contact us.

We publish poetry collections, short story collections, novellas and novels.

contact@thewriteorder.com

Instagram- thewriteorder

www.facebook.com/thewriteorder

www.ingramcontent.com/pod-product-compliance
Lightning Source LLC
LaVergne TN
LVHW021223080526
838199LV00089B/5818